Table Of Contents

Chapter 5: Producing High-Quality Videos

- Selecting the right equipment and software
- Filming techniques, lighting, and composition
- Editing tips for polished and professional videos

Chapter 6: Crafting Captivating Thumbnails and Titles

- The importance of thumbnails and titles
- Design principles for attention-grabbing thumbnails
- Writing click-worthy and SEO-friendly titles

Chapter 7: Mastering SEO and Keywords

- Understanding YouTube's search and discovery system
- Conducting keyword research for your videos
- Optimizing video descriptions, tags, and closed captions

Chapter 8: Uploading and Publishing Your Videos

- Uploading videos with proper settings
- Utilizing publishing options strategically
- Engaging with your audience through comments

Chapter 9: Building a Loyal Audience

- Consistency as a key factor in audience retention
- Encouraging viewers to subscribe and hit the notification bell
- Using end screens and cards effectively

Chapter 10: Promoting Your Channel and Videos

- Leveraging social media for cross-promotion
- Collaborating with other YouTubers and influencers
- Running targeted advertising campaigns

Chapter 11: Engaging with Your Community

- Maintaining ethical content creation practices
- Upholding YouTube's community standards

Chapter 18: The Future of YouTube and Adaptation

- Embracing evolving trends and formats
- Staying adaptable in a rapidly changing landscape
- Continued learning and growth as a creator

Conclusion: Your Journey to YouTube Stardom

- Reflecting on your progress and achievements
- Celebrating milestones and successes
- Embracing the ongoing journey of YouTube success

Appendix:

- Glossary of YouTube-related terms
- Recommended resources and tools for creators
- Worksheets for goal setting, content planning, and more

Chapter 1: Introduction to YouTube Success

Welcome to the exciting world of YouTube, where creativity, connection, and content come together to shape the digital landscape. In this chapter, we'll lay the foundation for your journey to YouTube success by understanding the immense power and potential of the platform. We'll delve into the importance of defining your niche and target audience, as well as setting realistic goals that will guide your channel's growth.

Understanding the Power and Potential of YouTube

YouTube is more than just a video-sharing platform; it's a global community that reaches billions of viewers daily. With over a billion hours of content watched every day, YouTube offers an unparalleled opportunity for creators to share their passions, expertise, and stories with the world. From entertainment to education, from vlogs to tutorials, YouTube has become a virtual space where people gather to learn, be entertained, and connect.

As a creator, you have the power to make a lasting impact, influence opinions, and build a dedicated audience. YouTube provides a stage where your creativity can shine, your voice can be heard, and your brand can flourish.

Defining Your Niche and Target Audience

One of the most critical steps in achieving YouTube success is defining your niche and identifying your target audience. Your niche is your area of expertise or the topic you're passionate about. Choosing a niche that aligns with your interests and skills will not only make creating content more enjoyable but also attract like-minded viewers.

When defining your niche, consider what you're knowledgeable about, what excites you, and what you can provide unique insights into. Whether it's cooking, fitness, technology, beauty, gaming, or any other topic, make sure it's something you're genuinely enthusiastic about.

After defining your niche, it's crucial to identify your target audience. Who are the people you want to reach with your content? What are their interests, demographics, and preferences? Tailoring your content to resonate with your target audience will increase engagement and foster a sense of community around your channel.

Setting Realistic Goals for Your Channel

As you embark on your YouTube journey, it's essential to set realistic goals that will guide your efforts and measure your progress. These goals can be short-term (e.g., reaching a certain number of subscribers in a month) or long-term (e.g., achieving a specific view count within a year). Your goals should be specific, measurable, achievable, relevant, and time-bound (SMART).

Remember that YouTube success is a gradual process. Building a loyal audience, gaining subscribers, and achieving significant views take time and dedication. Focus on creating high-quality content and nurturing your community rather than solely fixating on numbers. By setting achievable goals and staying committed to your vision, you'll be well on your way to building a successful YouTube channel.

In this chapter, you've laid the groundwork for your YouTube journey. You've learned about the incredible potential of the platform, the importance of defining your niche and audience, and the significance of setting realistic goals. As you move forward, keep these fundamental principles in mind—they'll serve as the building blocks for your path to YouTube success.

Chapter 2: Finding Your Passion and Niche

In this chapter, we'll delve into the process of discovering your passion, identifying your niche, and researching popular trends that align with your interests. Utilizing various tools and methods, you'll be able to make informed decisions about the direction of your YouTube channel.

Discovering Your Interests and Expertise

Start by exploring your personal interests, hobbies, and areas of expertise. Reflect on what makes you truly passionate and excited. This could be anything from cooking and fitness to technology and travel. List down your hobbies, skills, and experiences that could potentially become the foundation of your channel's content.

Researching Popular Niches and Trends

In order to establish a successful YouTube channel, it's essential to choose a niche that resonates with your interests and aligns with current trends. Conducting thorough research will help you make informed decisions about the direction of your content. Here's a step-by-step guide to researching popular niches and trends:

1. Brainstorm Your Interests: Start by making a list of topics that genuinely interest you. These could be hobbies, skills, passions, or areas of expertise that you're excited to share with others.

2. Use YouTube Search: Begin your research by typing keywords related to your interests into the YouTube search bar. Pay attention to the autocomplete suggestions that appear as you type, as these can provide insights into popular search queries. Take note of the types of videos that come up in the search results.

3. Explore Trending Videos: Visit the "Trending" section on YouTube to see which videos are currently popular. While not all trending topics may align with your niche, this will give you an overview of what's capturing viewers' attention across various categories.

4. Analyze View Counts and Engagement: Watch videos in your potential niche and analyze their view counts, likes, dislikes, comments, and shares. This will give you an idea of the demand for content in that niche and the level of engagement it generates.

5. Use Google Trends: Google Trends is a powerful tool that allows you to track the popularity of search queries over time. Compare different keywords related to your potential niche to identify patterns and see if interest is growing or declining.

6. Explore Social Media: Check social media platforms such as Instagram, Twitter, and TikTok to see what topics and content styles are gaining traction. Social media trends often influence YouTube content creation.

7. Keyword Research Tools: Utilize keyword research tools like Google Keyword Planner, Ubersuggest, or Ahrefs to identify keywords related to your niche. These tools provide data on search volume, competition, and related keywords.

8. Analyze Competitors: Identify successful YouTube channels within your potential niche. Study their content, engagement metrics, and subscriber counts. This can help you understand what works well in that niche and identify gaps you can fill with your unique content.

9. Consider Longevity: While it's important to ride the wave of current trends, consider the long-term viability of your chosen niche. Some trends might be fleeting, while others have more lasting appeal.

10. Evaluate Audience Demand: Ultimately, the success of your channel depends on the demand for your content. Ask yourself if there's a genuine audience interested in the niche you're considering.

Remember that striking a balance between your passion and the current trends is key. By conducting thorough research, you'll be better equipped to choose a niche that not only aligns with your interests but also has the potential to attract a dedicated and engaged audience.

Identifying Your Unique Value Proposition

In a vast sea of content on YouTube, your unique value proposition (UVP) is what sets you apart and makes your channel compelling to viewers. It's the distinct combination of your personality, expertise, and approach that resonates with your audience. Here's how to identify and develop your UVP:

1. Self-Reflection: Take some time to reflect on what makes you unique as a creator. Consider your skills, experiences, background, and personality traits that can contribute to your content. What do you bring to the table that others don't?

2. Define Your Niche Within the Niche: Even within a broader niche, there are sub-niches that allow for specialization. Identify the specific angle or aspect you want to focus on within your chosen niche. This specialization can become a part of your UVP.

3. Audience Perspective: Put yourself in your audience's shoes. What value do they seek when watching content in your niche? How can you address their needs, solve their problems, or entertain them uniquely?

4. Uncover Your Strengths: Identify your strengths as a creator. Are you an expert in a particular area? Do you have a talent for storytelling, humor, teaching, or connecting with people emotionally? Leverage these strengths in your content.

5. Authenticity and Personality: Your authenticity is a significant part of your UVP. Be yourself and let your personality shine through in your videos. Authenticity builds trust and helps viewers connect with you on a deeper level.

6. Differentiate from Competitors: Research other creators in your niche and understand what they offer. Identify gaps or aspects that you can provide differently or more effectively. Your UVP should fill these gaps.

7. Solve a Problem or Fulfill a Need: Think about the problems your target audience faces or the needs they have. How can your content address these challenges? Offering solutions or guidance can be a crucial part of your UVP.

8. Fresh Perspective: Consider how you can provide a fresh perspective on common topics. Is there a unique angle, innovative approach, or untapped aspect you can explore within your niche?

9. Consistency and Reliability: Consistency in content delivery and quality establishes reliability. When viewers know what to expect from your channel, they're more likely to subscribe and engage with your content.

10. Evolving and Improving: Your UVP may evolve over time as you gain experience and connect with your audience. Continuously assess and refine your UVP based on feedback and insights.

Remember that your UVP should be genuine and aligned with your passion. It's the driving force behind why viewers should choose your channel over others. As you develop your UVP, keep in mind that building a successful channel takes time, so stay patient, authentic, and open to growth. Your unique voice and perspective are what will ultimately make your channel stand out and thrive on YouTube.

Chapter 3: Planning Your Content Strategy

Crafting a successful YouTube channel requires more than just uploading videos randomly. A well-thought-out content strategy is your roadmap to consistency, growth, and engagement. In this chapter, we'll delve into the essential aspects of planning your content strategy, including creating a content calendar, brainstorming video ideas, and striking the right balance between variety and consistency.

Creating a Content Calendar

A content calendar is your organizational tool for scheduling and managing your video uploads. It helps you maintain consistency and avoid last-minute rushes. Here's how to create an effective content calendar:

1. **Choose a Schedule:** Decide how often you'll upload videos. Whether it's once a week, twice a month, or any other frequency, consistency is key.
2. **Identify Key Dates:** Note down important dates, holidays, or events that align with your niche. Creating content around these dates can increase relevance and engagement.
3. **Batch Filming and Editing:** Plan to film and edit multiple videos in one session. This can save time and ensure a steady flow of content.
4. **Plan Ahead:** Map out your content for the next few weeks or months. This allows you to anticipate upcoming videos and gather necessary resources.
5. **Use Digital Tools:** Utilize tools like Google Calendar, Trello, or specialized content calendar apps to manage and visualize your content plan.

Brainstorming Video Ideas

Brainstorming is a creative process that fuels the heart of your YouTube content. It's the gateway to crafting engaging and exciting videos that resonate with your audience. Here's a comprehensive guide to help you master the art of brainstorming video ideas:

1. Define Your Goals: Understand what you want to achieve with your channel. Are you educating, entertaining, inspiring, or a combination of these? Your goals will guide your brainstorming process.

2. Know Your Audience: Identify your target audience's preferences, interests, and pain points. What questions do they have? What challenges do they face? Tailor your video ideas to meet their needs.

3. Embrace Your Niche: Stay true to your niche while exploring its various aspects. This ensures your content remains relevant and resonates with your dedicated audience.

4. Research and Trends: Stay informed about trends and viral topics within your niche. Utilize tools like Google Trends, social media, and content aggregators to identify popular topics.

5. Solve Problems: Create videos that offer solutions to common problems or challenges your audience might be experiencing. How-to guides, tutorials, and step-by-step demonstrations can be highly valuable.

6. Share Personal Experiences: Infuse authenticity by sharing personal stories, experiences, and insights related to your niche. Personal anecdotes can build a strong connection with your audience.

7. Explainer Videos: Break down complex concepts, terms, or processes related to your niche. Explainer videos can make your content more accessible to a wider audience.

8. Reviews and Recommendations: Review products, services, books, movies, or anything relevant to your niche. Provide honest opinions and recommendations to help your audience make informed choices.

9. Behind-the-Scenes: Take your audience behind the scenes of your content creation process. Show them your setup, editing process, and the effort that goes into making your videos.

10. Collaborations: Team up with other YouTubers or experts in your niche for collaborative videos. Collaborations can introduce your channel to new audiences and bring fresh perspectives.

11. Challenges and Experiments: Engage your audience by taking on challenges or experiments related to your niche. It could be trying out new techniques, testing products, or exploring uncharted territory.

12. Q&A Sessions: Host Q&A sessions where you answer questions from your audience. This fosters engagement and allows you to address their specific concerns.

13. Predict the Future: Share your insights and predictions about future trends, advancements, or developments within your niche. This establishes you as an authority in your field.

14. Holiday and Seasonal Content: Create videos around holidays, seasons, or relevant events. Tailor your content to fit the theme and capitalize on timely topics.

15. Educational Series: Design a series of videos that delve deep into a specific topic within your niche. This can encourage viewers to binge-watch and engage with your content.

16. Trend Adaptation: Adapt trending challenges, memes, or concepts to fit your niche. This combines popular trends with your expertise, creating a unique fusion.

17. Day in the Life: Give your audience a glimpse into your daily routine, work process, or a typical day in your life. This personal touch can humanize your content.

Remember, the most successful video ideas often stem from a blend of creativity, audience understanding, and a genuine passion for your niche. Keep a notebook or digital document handy to jot down ideas as they come to you. With consistent brainstorming, your content well will never run dry, and your YouTube channel will thrive with engaging and valuable videos.

Here are some tools and platforms you can use to find video ideas for your YouTube channel:

1. **YouTube Search and Autocomplete:** Start by typing keywords related to your niche into the YouTube search bar. As you type, YouTube's autocomplete feature will suggest popular search queries, giving you insights into what people are searching for.
2. **YouTube Trending:** The "Trending" section on YouTube showcases videos that are currently popular. While not all trending topics may fit your niche, exploring this section can give you a sense of what's capturing viewers' attention.
3. **Google Trends:** Google Trends allows you to compare the popularity of different search terms over time. You can identify rising topics, compare keywords, and see regional interest. This can help you align your content with current trends.
4. **Keyword Research Tools:**
    - **Google Keyword Planner:** While primarily designed for advertisers, this tool provides insights into keyword search volume and related terms.
    - **Ubersuggest:** Offers keyword suggestions, search volume, and SEO difficulty for your chosen keywords.

- **Answer The Public:** Generates visual representations of questions and phrases related to a keyword, helping you brainstorm content ideas.

5. **Social Media Platforms:** Platforms like Twitter, Instagram, and TikTok can offer insights into trending topics and discussions. Use relevant hashtags and follow influencers to stay updated.

6. **Quora:** Browse through Quora's questions and answers related to your niche. Pay attention to questions that have high engagement to identify topics of interest.

7. **BuzzSumo:** This tool allows you to search for popular topics and content in your niche. You can see which articles and videos are getting shared the most.

8. **Reddit:** Explore relevant subreddits to see what discussions are gaining traction. Subreddits related to your niche can be a goldmine for content ideas.

1. **Social Media Listening Tools:** Tools like Brandwatch, Hootsuite, or Mention can help you track conversations, trends, and discussions related to your niche on various social media platforms.

1. **Competitor Analysis:** Study successful YouTube channels in your niche. Analyze their most popular videos, comments, and audience engagement to get inspiration for your own content.

2. **Online Forums and Communities:** Platforms like forums, Facebook Groups, and LinkedIn Groups can provide insights into the questions and concerns people have within your niche.

3. **BuzzFeed:** Check out BuzzFeed's various sections and lists to see what types of content are popular and generating engagement.

4. **Google News:** Stay updated with the latest news and events within your niche using Google News. Current events can inspire timely and relevant content.

5. **Industry Publications:** Look for industry-specific magazines, blogs, and websites. They often cover trending topics and emerging issues that you can translate into video content.

Balancing Variety and Consistency

Finding the right balance between variety and consistency is crucial. While consistency keeps your audience engaged, variety ensures that your content remains fresh and appealing. Here's how to strike that balance:

1. **Content Themes:** While maintaining a consistent theme within your niche, diversify your content by exploring different angles, formats, and styles.
2. **Series and Segments:** Introduce recurring series or segments that your audience can look forward to. This adds predictability while allowing for creative variations.
3. **Content Mix:** Alternate between different types of content, such as tutorials, vlogs, reviews, and behind-the-scenes videos. This keeps your channel dynamic.
4. **Feedback and Analytics:** Pay attention to audience feedback and video analytics. Adjust your content strategy based on what resonates with your viewers.
5. **Planning Ahead:** When brainstorming video ideas, consider planning multiple videos at once. This way, you can ensure variety while maintaining your upload schedule.

Creating a content calendar, brainstorming diverse video ideas, and balancing consistency with variety are integral parts of your content strategy. As you put these strategies into practice, you'll be well on your way to providing valuable content that engages your audience and fuels the growth of your YouTube channel.

Chapter 4: Setting Up Your YouTube Channel

Your YouTube channel is your digital identity and the first impression viewers have of your content. In this chapter, we'll explore the crucial steps to set up your YouTube channel for success, including creating a compelling channel name and branding, designing an eye-catching channel banner and logo, and writing an engaging channel description.

Creating a Compelling Channel Name and Branding

Your channel name is the cornerstone of your brand identity on YouTube. It should be memorable, relevant to your content, and easy to spell. Here's how to choose a compelling channel name:

1. **Relevance:** Ensure that your channel name reflects the essence of your content and niche. It should give viewers a clear idea of what to expect.

2. **Memorability:** Choose a name that is easy to remember and doesn't contain unnecessary numbers or special characters.

3. **Uniqueness:** Research existing channel names to avoid duplication. You want a name that stands out and is distinguishable from others.

4. **Future-Proofing:** Consider whether your channel name will still be relevant as your content evolves or expands in the future.

5. **Consistency:** Try to align your channel name with your social media handles for consistency across platforms.

Designing an Eye-Catching Channel Banner and Logo

Your channel banner and logo are visual elements that represent your brand and capture viewers' attention. They should reflect your content's style and niche. Here's how to design compelling visuals:

1. **Channel Banner:** Create a banner that includes your channel name, tagline, and a brief description of your content. Use high-quality images that convey the tone of your videos.

2. **Logo:** Design a simple and recognizable logo that can be used across platforms. It should be versatile and easily identifiable even at smaller sizes.

3. **Color Palette:** Choose a color palette that resonates with your content's theme and evokes the right emotions. Consistency in colors helps establish your brand identity.

4. **Typography:** Select fonts that are legible and reflect your content's style. Use different fonts for headings, subheadings, and body text to add hierarchy.

5. **Professionalism:** Invest in professional design tools or seek assistance from graphic designers if you're not confident in your design skills.

Writing an Engaging Channel Description

Your channel description is where you introduce yourself to potential subscribers and tell them what your content is all about. Here's how to craft an engaging channel description:

1. **Introduction:** Start with a brief introduction about yourself and what viewers can expect from your channel.
2. **Niche and Content:** Clearly explain your niche and the types of videos you'll be creating. Highlight your unique angle or approach within the niche.
3. **Value Proposition:** Explain the value viewers will get from subscribing to your channel. What will they learn, enjoy, or experience by watching your videos?
4. **Call to Action:** Encourage viewers to subscribe, like, comment, and share your videos. Let them know why being part of your community is worthwhile.
5. **Keywords:** Include relevant keywords in your description to improve discoverability in search results.
6. **Links:** Add links to your social media profiles, website, and any other relevant platforms to help viewers connect with you outside of YouTube.

Setting up your YouTube channel involves more than just technical details; it's about crafting a brand identity that resonates with your audience. By carefully choosing your channel name, designing eye-catching visuals, and writing an engaging channel description, you're laying the foundation for a memorable and impactful presence on YouTube.

Chapter 5: Producing High-Quality Videos

The quality of your videos plays a pivotal role in capturing your audience's attention and keeping them engaged. In this chapter, we'll explore the essential elements of producing high-quality videos, including selecting the right equipment and software, mastering filming techniques, optimizing lighting and composition, and using editing tips for polished and professional content.

Selecting the Right Equipment and Software

Investing in the right equipment and software can significantly enhance the quality of your videos. Here's what you need to consider:

1. **Camera:** While a high-end camera is ideal, smartphones with good camera capabilities can also produce excellent results. Choose one with good resolution and manual settings.

- Canon EOS M50 Mark II
- Sony A6400
- Panasonic Lumix GH5

1. **Microphone:** High-quality audio is crucial. Consider using an external microphone for clearer sound. Options include shotgun mics, lapel mics, and USB microphones.

- Rode VideoMic Pro
- Audio-Technica AT2020 USB microphone
- Zoom H5 Handy Recorder (for external audio recording)

1. **Tripod or Stabilizer:** Avoid shaky footage by using a tripod or stabilizer. This ensures your videos look steady and professional.

- Manfrotto PIXI Mini Tripod
- DJI Osmo Mobile 4 Gimbal Stabilizer

1. **Lighting Equipment:** Invest in basic lighting equipment, like softboxes or ring lights, to ensure consistent and flattering lighting in your videos.
   - Neewer 18-inch Ring Light Kit
   - Godox SL-60W LED Video Light
2. **Video Editing Software:** Choose user-friendly video editing software that suits your needs. Popular options include Adobe Premiere Pro, Final Cut Pro, and even free tools like DaVinci Resolve.

Online Tools:

1. **Video Editing:**
   - Adobe Premiere Pro
   - Final Cut Pro X (Mac only)
   - DaVinci Resolve (free version available)
   - HitFilm Express (free version available)
2. **Audio Editing:**
   - Adobe Audition
   - Audacity (free and open-source)
3. **Graphic Design:**
   - Adobe Photoshop (for creating channel art and thumbnails)
   - Canva (user-friendly online design tool)
4. **Color Grading:**
   - Adobe After Effects (for advanced color correction and grading)
   - DaVinci Resolve (includes powerful color grading tools)
5. **Screen Recording and Capture:**
   - OBS Studio (free and open-source screen recording and streaming)
   - Camtasia (for screen recording and video editing)
6. **Animation and Motion Graphics:**
   - Adobe After Effects (for creating animations and motion graphics)
   - Blender (free and open-source 3D animation software)

Filming Techniques, Lighting, and Composition

Mastering filming techniques and understanding lighting and composition are essential for creating visually appealing videos-

Filming Techniques:

1. **Steady Shots:** Use a tripod or stabilizer to avoid shaky footage. Stable shots enhance the overall professionalism of your videos.
2. **Variety of Angles:** Experiment with different camera angles to add visual interest. Use wide shots, close-ups, and creative perspectives to enhance storytelling.
3. **Rule of Thirds:** Imagine your frame divided into nine equal sections using two horizontal and two vertical lines. Position key elements along these lines or at their intersections for balanced composition.
4. **Depth and Layering:** Create depth by including foreground, midground, and background elements in your shots. This adds dimension and visual complexity.
5. **Movement with Purpose:** Use camera movement purposefully. Panning, tilting, and tracking shots can emphasize details or guide the viewer's attention.

Lighting:

1. **Soft Lighting:** Use soft lighting sources like diffused window light, softboxes, or ring lights. Soft lighting minimizes harsh shadows and produces flattering results.
2. **Three-Point Lighting:** Employ a three-point lighting setup: key light (main light), fill light (reduces shadows), and backlight (separates subject from the background).
3. **Golden Hour:** If shooting outdoors, capture footage during the golden hours—shortly after sunrise or before sunset—when natural lighting is soft and warm.
4. **Avoid Overexposure and Underexposure:** Maintain a balance between highlights and shadows. Avoid blown-out areas (too bright) and areas with no detail (too dark).

5. **Color Temperature:** Ensure consistent color temperature across all your lights. Avoid mixing warm and cool lights in the same shot.

Composition:

1. **Rule of Thirds:** Place your subject or key elements along the lines or intersections of the imaginary grid for a balanced and visually pleasing composition.

2. **Centered Composition:** Centering your subject can create a balanced and symmetrical look. Use this technique when you want a strong focal point.

3. **Leading Lines:** Utilize natural lines, such as roads, pathways, or architectural features, to guide the viewer's eye toward the subject.

4. **Frame Within a Frame:** Incorporate elements within the scene, like doorways or windows, to create a natural frame around the subject.

5. **Negative Space:** Use negative space (empty areas) intentionally to emphasize your subject and give the viewer's eyes a resting place.

6. **Symmetry and Asymmetry:** Experiment with both symmetrical and asymmetrical compositions. Symmetry can create a sense of order, while asymmetry adds dynamic energy.

Editing Tips for Polished and Professional Videos

Editing is where your raw footage transforms into a polished final product. Here are editing tips to elevate your videos:

1. **Trimming and Cutting:** Remove unnecessary parts of your footage to maintain a smooth flow. Keep your videos concise and engaging.
2. **Transitions:** Use smooth transitions between clips to create a seamless viewing experience. Avoid overly flashy transitions that can be distracting.
3. **Color Correction and Grading:** Adjust colors, brightness, and contrast to achieve a consistent and visually pleasing look. Use color grading to set the mood of your videos.
4. **Audio Enhancement:** Remove background noise, balance audio levels, and add music or sound effects to enhance the overall audio experience.
5. **Graphics and Text:** Add graphics, text overlays, and subtitles to provide context, emphasize points, and improve viewer engagement.
6. **Pacing and B-Roll:** Maintain a good pacing by interspersing main content with relevant B-roll footage. B-roll adds depth and visual interest.

By mastering the art of producing high-quality videos, you're not only enhancing the viewer's experience but also building your reputation as a skilled content creator. The right equipment, filming techniques, lighting, and editing skills will contribute to videos that captivate your audience and leave a lasting impression.

Chapter 6: Crafting Captivating Thumbnails and Titles

Your video's thumbnails and titles are the first things viewers see, making them crucial in attracting clicks and setting expectations. In this chapter, we'll explore the significance of thumbnails and titles, delve into design principles for attention-grabbing thumbnails, and learn how to write click-worthy and SEO-friendly titles.

The Importance of Thumbnails and Titles

Thumbnails and titles serve as a dynamic duo that entices viewers to click and watch your videos. They provide a sneak peek into your content and influence whether a viewer decides to watch. Here's why they matter:

1. **First Impressions:** Thumbnails and titles are the first elements viewers encounter, influencing their decision to click or scroll past.
2. **Curiosity and Expectations:** A well-crafted thumbnail and title can spark curiosity and set expectations about what the video offers.
3. **Search and Recommendations:** Thumbnails and titles impact your video's visibility in search results and recommendation algorithms.

Design Principles for Attention-Grabbing Thumbnails

Creating thumbnails that stand out requires thoughtful design. Keep these principles in mind:

1. **Clarity and Focus:** Ensure your thumbnail clearly conveys the video's topic or content. Use one central element as the focal point.
2. **Contrasting Colors:** Use contrasting colors to make your thumbnail elements pop. A bold color scheme can grab attention amid a sea of thumbnails.
3. **Engaging Facial Expressions:** If your video features people, use expressive facial close-ups to evoke emotions and create a connection.

4. **Text Overlay:** Add concise text to highlight key points or benefits of the video. Choose readable fonts and ensure text is legible on different devices.

5. **Simplicity:** Avoid cluttering the thumbnail with too many elements. A clean, simple design is more visually appealing.

6. **Consistency:** Maintain a consistent visual style for your thumbnails to establish brand recognition. Use similar fonts, colors, and layouts.

Writing Click-Worthy and SEO-Friendly Titles

Crafting titles that entice clicks while optimizing for search engines requires a strategic approach:

1. **Keyword Research:** Research relevant keywords related to your video's topic. Use tools like Google Keyword Planner and YouTube's search suggest feature.

2. **Clear and Compelling:** Create titles that clearly communicate what viewers can expect. Make them intriguing without being misleading.

3. **Length:** Keep titles concise and under 60 characters to prevent truncation in search results. Front-load important information.

4. **Include Keywords:** Incorporate your primary keyword naturally in the title. This improves search visibility and relevancy.

5. **Audience-Centric:** Consider what your target audience is looking for. Address their pain points or provide solutions in your titles.

6. **Curiosity and Benefit:** Spark curiosity by leaving some information unsaid, encouraging viewers to click to learn more.

7. **A/B Testing:** Experiment with different titles for similar videos to see which ones generate better click-through rates.

By mastering the art of crafting captivating thumbnails and titles, you can significantly boost your video's click-through rate and engagement. Remember, thumbnails and titles are your video's virtual storefront; they need to be enticing, informative, and reflective of your content's quality and value.

Chapter 7: Mastering SEO and Keywords

Search Engine Optimization (SEO) plays a crucial role in making your videos discoverable on YouTube. In this chapter, we'll dive into understanding YouTube's search and discovery system, conducting effective keyword research, and optimizing your video descriptions, tags, and closed captions for maximum visibility.

Understanding YouTube's Search and Discovery System

YouTube's search and discovery system determines how videos are ranked and recommended to users. Key factors include user engagement, watch time, and relevance. Here's how it works:

1. **User Engagement:** Videos that receive more clicks, likes, shares, and comments are seen as engaging and are more likely to be recommended.
2. **Watch Time:** Longer watch times signal to YouTube that your content is valuable and relevant. Videos with higher watch times are given priority.
3. **Relevance:** YouTube analyzes your video's metadata (title, description, tags, and closed captions) to understand its content and context.

Conducting Keyword Research for Your Videos

Keyword research is a critical step in optimizing your videos for search and discovery on YouTube. Here's a detailed guide on how to conduct effective keyword research:

1. Brainstorm Relevant Keywords: Start by brainstorming keywords and phrases related to your video's topic. Think about what your target audience might search for when looking for content like yours. Write down a list of potential keywords.

2. Utilize YouTube's Search Suggest: Head to the YouTube search bar and begin typing your main keywords. YouTube's auto-suggest feature will provide you with additional keyword ideas that are popular among users.

3. Analyze Competitor Videos: Search for similar videos in your niche and analyze their titles, descriptions, and tags. This can give you insights into the keywords your competitors are targeting.

4. Use Keyword Research Tools: Employ keyword research tools to get comprehensive data on search volume, competition, and related keywords. Some useful tools include:

- **Google Keyword Planner:** Provides data on search volume and suggests relevant keywords.
- **Ubersuggest:** Offers keyword suggestions, search volume, and difficulty scores.
- **TubeBuddy:** YouTube-focused tool that provides keyword insights and competition analysis.
- **VidIQ:** Similar to TubeBuddy, offering keyword recommendations and search analytics.

5. Long-Tail Keywords: Consider using long-tail keywords—phrases containing three or more words. These keywords might have lower search volume but can be more specific and less competitive.

6. Focus on Relevance: Choose keywords that are highly relevant to your video's content. Avoid using unrelated or misleading keywords, as this can negatively impact your video's performance and viewer experience.

7. Balance Broad and Specific Keywords: Include a mix of broad keywords that cover your video's general topic and specific keywords that target niche aspects of your content.

8. Analyze Search Intent: Consider the intent behind the keyword. Is the viewer looking for information, a tutorial, a review, or entertainment? Tailor your content to match the viewer's intent.

9. Prioritize Low Competition Keywords: While high-volume keywords are attractive, they often come with high competition. Prioritize keywords with a reasonable search volume and lower competition to increase your chances of ranking.

10. Monitor Trends: Keep an eye on trending topics and keywords within your niche. Creating timely content around trending keywords can boost your video's visibility.

11. Refine Over Time: Regularly review and refine your keyword strategy based on changes in search trends, audience preferences, and the performance of your videos.

Optimizing Video Descriptions, Tags, and Closed Captions

Optimizing your video's metadata helps YouTube understand your content and rank it accurately:

1. **Video Title:** Include your primary keyword naturally within the first 60 characters of your title. Make it engaging and concise.
2. **Video Description:** Write a detailed, informative description that includes your target keywords. Front-load important information and provide context.

- **Include Keywords:** Incorporate your primary keyword naturally in the video description. Provide a brief summary of what the video is about.
- **Detailed Description:** Write a comprehensive description that provides context about the content. Include relevant keywords and phrases related to the video's topic.

- **Front-Load Information:** Place important information and keywords near the beginning of the description to capture viewers' attention.
- **Call to Action (CTA):** Encourage viewers to like, comment, subscribe, and share your video. Include links to your website or social media if relevant.
- **Timestamps:** If your video covers multiple topics, include timestamps in the description. This helps viewers navigate to specific sections of the video.

1. **Tags:** Add relevant tags that describe your video's content. Use a mix of broad and specific tags. Include variations and synonyms of your main keyword.

- **Relevant and Specific Tags:** Add tags that accurately describe your video's content. Use a mix of broad and specific tags to capture different search queries.
- **Primary Keyword:** Include your primary keyword as a tag. This helps YouTube understand the topic of your video.
- **Variations and Synonyms:** Use variations and synonyms of your main keyword as additional tags. This increases the likelihood of your video appearing in various searches.
- **Long-Tail Tags:** Include long-tail tags that reflect specific aspects of your video. Long-tail tags can target niche audiences.

1. **Closed Captions (CC):** Upload accurate and well-formatted closed captions. Closed captions not only improve accessibility but also provide additional metadata for search algorithms.

- **Accurate Captions:** Ensure your closed captions are accurate and well-synced with the audio. Incorrect captions can lead to a negative viewer experience.
- **Transcriptions:** Provide a full transcript of the video in the closed captions. This enhances accessibility and improves search visibility.
- **Include Keywords:** Naturally include relevant keywords in your closed captions. YouTube uses closed captions for indexing and ranking.
- **Keywords in Opening Moments:** Place important keywords in the opening moments of the video to improve search visibility.

- **Edit and Review:** Review and edit auto-generated captions for accuracy. Incorrect captions can impact search rankings and viewer satisfaction.

1. **Playlists:** Organize your videos into relevant playlists. Playlists improve user engagement and encourage longer watch times.
2. **End Screens and Cards:** Use end screens and cards to promote other relevant videos on your channel. This encourages viewers to continue watching your content.
3. **Engagement Signals:** Encourage likes, comments, shares, and subscriptions in your videos. Engagement signals tell YouTube that your content is valuable.

By mastering SEO and keywords, you can enhance your video's visibility and increase the likelihood of reaching a broader audience. Remember, optimization is an ongoing process; regularly review and refine your strategies based on analytics and trends. As you consistently provide relevant, high-quality content, YouTube's search and discovery system will work in your favor, driving more views and engagement to your videos.

Chapter 8: Uploading and Publishing Your Videos

Uploading and publishing your videos on YouTube is the final step before sharing your content with the world. In this chapter, we'll explore the essential aspects of uploading videos with proper settings, utilizing publishing options strategically, and engaging with your audience through comments.

Uploading Videos with Proper Settings

1. **Video Format:** Use common video formats like MP4, MOV, or AVI. YouTube also supports HD and 4K resolutions for high-quality playback.
2. **Resolution and Aspect Ratio:** Opt for resolutions that match your recording quality (e.g., 1080p, 720p) and maintain the correct aspect ratio (16:9 is standard).
3. **Video Title and Description:** Enter a clear and descriptive title that includes your main keyword. Craft a detailed description that provides context about your video's content.
4. **Tags and Closed Captions:** Add relevant tags to help YouTube understand your video's topic. Include accurate closed captions for improved accessibility.
5. **Thumbnail:** Upload an attention-grabbing thumbnail that accurately represents your video's content and intrigues potential viewers.
6. **Visibility:** Choose your video's visibility settings. You can set it as "Public" to make it accessible to everyone, or schedule it for future release.

Utilizing Publishing Options Strategically

1. **Publishing Time:** Consider your target audience's time zone and habits when scheduling your video's release time. Peak viewing hours can lead to higher initial engagement.

2. **Premieres:** Use the premiere feature to create anticipation. Premieres allow you to schedule a live chat with viewers before your video goes live.

3. **End Screens and Cards:** Add end screens and cards to promote other videos, encourage subscriptions, and keep viewers engaged after the video ends.

4. **Playlists:** Organize your videos into playlists to encourage longer viewing sessions. Playlists enhance user experience and boost watch time.

5. **Monetization and Ads:** If eligible, choose whether to enable ads on your videos. This can generate revenue, but ensure ads don't disrupt the viewer's experience.

Engaging with Your Audience Through Comments

1. **Respond to Comments:** Engage with your audience by responding to comments on your videos. This builds a sense of community and encourages further interaction.

2. **Moderate Comments:** Monitor and moderate comments to ensure a positive and respectful environment for your viewers.

3. **Feedback and Interaction:** Encourage viewers to share their thoughts, ideas, and feedback in the comments. Respond to questions and address concerns.

4. **Pin Important Comments:** Pin comments that provide valuable information or foster meaningful discussions. This keeps them visible to all viewers.

5. **Viewer Suggestions:** Pay attention to viewer suggestions and requests for future content. This can provide inspiration for your upcoming videos.

By uploading videos with proper settings, strategically utilizing publishing options, and engaging with your audience through comments, you're fostering a strong connection with your viewers. Your interaction not only enhances the viewer experience but also helps you understand your audience's preferences, improving the quality and relevance of your content over time.

Chapter 9: Building a Loyal Audience

Building a loyal and engaged audience is crucial for long-term success on YouTube. In this chapter, we'll explore the essential strategies to cultivate a loyal audience, including maintaining consistency, encouraging subscriptions and notifications, and using end screens and cards effectively.

Consistency as a Key Factor in Audience Retention

1. **Regular Upload Schedule:** Stick to a consistent upload schedule that suits your content style and production capacity. Consistency helps viewers know when to expect new content.
2. **Quality Over Quantity:** While consistency is important, prioritize delivering high-quality content. It's better to maintain a consistent schedule of well-crafted videos than to sacrifice quality for frequent uploads.
3. **Themes and Series:** Introduce themes or series in your content. This creates anticipation and encourages viewers to return for more content on a specific topic.

Encouraging Viewers to Subscribe and Hit the Notification Bell

1. **Call to Action (CTA):** Politely remind viewers to subscribe to your channel and hit the notification bell to receive updates when you upload new content.
2. **Subscriber Benefits:** Highlight the value of subscribing, such as exclusive content, early access, or community perks.
3. **End of Videos:** Place a subscription CTA at the end of your videos when viewers are most engaged.

Using End Screens and Cards Effectively

1. **End Screens:** Utilize end screens to promote your other videos, playlists, and encourage subscriptions. Place them strategically to keep viewers engaged even after the video ends.
2. **Cards:** Add cards at specific moments in your videos to link to relevant content, including videos, playlists, websites, and merchandise.
3. **Interactive Elements:** Experiment with polls and quizzes through cards to increase viewer engagement and encourage participation.
4. **Personalized Recommendations:** Tailor end screens and cards to the content being watched, providing viewers with relevant options.

Engagement and Community Building

1. **Respond to Comments:** Engage with viewers by responding to comments promptly. Foster a positive and respectful environment for discussions.
2. **Ask for Input:** Involve your audience by asking for their opinions, ideas, and suggestions. This creates a sense of ownership and involvement.
3. **Live Streams and Q&A Sessions:** Host live streams or Q&A sessions to interact with your audience in real time. This deepens the connection and allows for immediate engagement.
4. **Shoutouts and Community Highlights:** Recognize and feature active and supportive members of your community in your videos or on social media.

Building a loyal audience requires dedication, patience, and genuine interaction. By being consistent, encouraging subscriptions and notifications, and effectively using end screens and cards, you're fostering a community that values your content and looks forward to your videos. Over time, this loyal audience can become advocates who help promote your channel and increase its reach.

Chapter 10: Promoting Your Channel and Videos

Promoting your channel and videos beyond YouTube's platform is essential for expanding your reach and attracting new viewers. In this chapter, we'll explore effective strategies to promote your content, including leveraging social media for cross-promotion, collaborating with other YouTubers and influencers, and running targeted advertising campaigns.

Leveraging Social Media for Cross-Promotion

Social media platforms offer valuable opportunities to expand your YouTube audience by promoting your content to a wider audience. Here's how to effectively leverage social media for cross-promotion:

1. Choose the Right Platforms: Identify the social media platforms that align with your content and target audience. Popular options include Instagram, Twitter, Facebook, TikTok, and LinkedIn.

2. Create Compelling Profiles: Optimize your social media profiles to reflect your YouTube channel's branding. Use a consistent profile picture, cover photo, and bio.

3. Share Teasers and Highlights: Create short teaser clips or highlight reels from your YouTube videos. These previews should be intriguing enough to encourage viewers to watch the full video on your channel.

4. Use Eye-Catching Visuals: Images and thumbnails matter. Use high-quality images, engaging graphics, and attention-grabbing thumbnails to make your posts stand out.

5. Write Engaging Captions: Craft captions that provide context, generate curiosity, and encourage interaction. Ask questions, share insights, or create a narrative that complements the video.

6. Utilize Hashtags: Research relevant hashtags related to your content and industry. Use them strategically in your posts to increase the discoverability of your content.

7. Platform-Specific Content: Tailor your content to each platform's format and audience expectations. For instance, Instagram Stories, Twitter threads, and TikTok videos have unique characteristics.

8. Schedule and Consistency: Maintain a consistent posting schedule to keep your audience engaged. Utilize social media scheduling tools to plan your posts in advance.

9. Engage with Your Audience: Respond to comments, questions, and messages from your audience. Engaging with your followers builds a sense of community and encourages further interaction.

10. Use Cross-Platform Sharing: When you publish a new YouTube video, share it across all your social media platforms. Include a link, eye-catching visuals, and a brief description.

11. Collaborate with Others: Collaborate with influencers, content creators, or brands on social media. These partnerships can help expose your content to a wider audience.

12. Utilize Stories and Live Videos: Use features like Stories and Live videos to showcase behind-the-scenes content, Q&A sessions, or updates about your channel.

13. Promote Special Content: Announce special events, giveaways, or exclusive content releases on social media to encourage engagement and excitement.

Collaborating with Other YouTubers and Influencers

Collaborations with other YouTubers and influencers can greatly expand your reach and introduce your content to new audiences. Here's how to effectively collaborate with others to promote your YouTube channel:

1. Find Compatible Partners: Identify content creators and influencers whose audience aligns with yours. Look for creators in your niche or related niches who share similar values and content style.

2. Research Their Content: Familiarize yourself with your potential collaborator's content. Understand their audience, engagement, and the type of content they create.

3. Choose Collaboration Types: Consider various collaboration formats, such as joint videos, challenges, interviews, or series. Choose an approach that suits both your content styles.

4. Approach with Value: When reaching out to potential collaborators, highlight how the collaboration can benefit both parties and their audiences. Emphasize the value you can bring.

5. Develop a Concept: Collaborate on an engaging and relevant concept that showcases both collaborators' strengths. The idea should provide value to both audiences.

6. Plan Logistics: Discuss details such as the video format, topic, length, recording schedule, and post-production tasks. Clear communication is essential.

7. Cross-Promotion: Promote the collaboration across your social media platforms and on your YouTube channel before the video release. This builds anticipation.

8. Execute the Collaboration: Record the collaborative content, ensuring both collaborators contribute equally and authentically. Focus on creating valuable content.

9. Edit and Post: Edit the video to maintain a consistent quality and style. Decide on the release date and ensure both collaborators are aligned.

10. Utilize CTAs: Encourage viewers to check out your collaborator's content and vice versa. Use end screens, cards, and descriptions to link to each other's channels.

11. Engage and Respond: When the collaborative video goes live, actively engage with the comments, responding to viewers from both audiences.

12. Monitor Results: Analyze the performance of the collaboration. Pay attention to views, engagement, and subscriber growth to gauge its impact.

13. Build Relationships: Collaborations are opportunities to build relationships in the YouTube community. Consider ongoing partnerships or collaborations with multiple creators.

14. Be Professional: Respect your collaborator's time and efforts. Communicate effectively, meet deadlines, and maintain a professional attitude throughout.

Collaborations introduce your content to a wider audience and allow you to tap into your collaborator's fan base. By focusing on creating valuable and engaging content together, you can attract new subscribers and viewers while also forming meaningful connections within the YouTube community.

Running Targeted Advertising Campaigns

1. **YouTube Ads:** Use YouTube's advertising platform to run ads that appear as suggested videos or in search results. Target specific demographics, interests, and keywords.
2. **Google Ads:** Utilize Google Ads to reach potential viewers across various websites and platforms through display ads and video ads.
3. **Social Media Ads:** Run ads on social media platforms like Facebook, Instagram, and Twitter to reach users who match your target audience.

Engaging with Promotional Strategies:

1. **Promotion Plan:** Develop a strategic promotion plan that outlines your goals, target audience, platforms, and content release schedule.
2. **Consistency:** Be consistent with your promotional efforts. Regularly share content, engage with your audience, and collaborate with others.
3. **Analyzing Results:** Monitor the performance of your promotional strategies using analytics tools. Adjust your approach based on data and feedback.

Promoting your channel and videos beyond YouTube is essential for attracting new viewers and growing your audience. By leveraging social media, collaborating with influencers, and running targeted advertising campaigns, you can increase your channel's visibility and reach a broader audience who may not have discovered your content otherwise.

Chapter 11: Engaging with Your Community

Engaging with your community is a vital aspect of building a loyal and active audience on YouTube. In this chapter, we'll delve into the strategies for effectively interacting with your audience, hosting live streams and Q&A sessions, and incorporating feedback to make continuous improvements.

Responding to Comments and Messages

1. **Timely Responses:** Regularly check and respond to comments on your videos. Engage with your viewers by thanking them for positive feedback and addressing their questions or opinions.
2. **Stay Positive:** Maintain a positive and respectful tone when responding to comments, even in the face of criticism. Constructive interactions enhance your channel's reputation.
3. **Engage in Discussions:** Foster discussions by replying to comments that spark conversation among viewers. Encourage viewers to share their thoughts and engage with each other.
4. **Pin Important Comments:** Pin comments that provide valuable insights or important information to ensure they're easily visible to all viewers.

Hosting Live Streams and Q&A Sessions

1. **Live Streams:** Host live streams to interact with your audience in real time. Discuss topics related to your content, answer questions, and engage in discussions.
2. **Q&A Sessions:** Conduct Q&A sessions where viewers can ask you questions about your channel, content, or personal experiences. This personal connection strengthens the bond with your audience.
3. **Announce in Advance:** Promote your live streams and Q&A sessions ahead of time to attract viewers and ensure a higher turnout.

4. **Encourage Interaction:** During live sessions, actively interact with viewers by addressing their questions, comments, and opinions. Create a dynamic and engaging atmosphere.

Listening to Audience Feedback and Making Improvements

1. **Feedback Channels:** Provide various channels for viewers to give feedback, such as comments, social media, and community posts. Let your audience know their opinions matter.
2. **Surveys and Polls:** Conduct surveys and polls to gather specific feedback on content ideas, video topics, and channel improvements.
3. **Feedback Analysis:** Regularly review and analyze audience feedback. Identify recurring themes, suggestions, and concerns.
4. **Adapt and Evolve:** Use audience feedback to make improvements to your content, video quality, production style, and overall channel strategy.
5. **Transparency:** If you're implementing changes based on feedback, communicate these changes to your audience. Demonstrating that you value their input builds trust.

Engaging with your community not only strengthens the bond between you and your audience but also improves your content's relevance and quality. By actively participating in discussions, hosting interactive sessions, and incorporating feedback, you create a space where viewers feel valued and invested in your channel's growth. Remember that audience engagement is an ongoing process that requires genuine interaction and a commitment to providing value to your viewers.

Chapter 12: Monetization and Revenue Streams

Monetizing your YouTube channel is an exciting step that allows you to turn your passion into a source of income. In this chapter, we'll cover the key aspects of monetization, including understanding YouTube's policies, exploring different revenue streams, and diversifying your income.

Understanding YouTube's Monetization Policies

Monetizing your YouTube channel involves adhering to specific policies set by YouTube to ensure quality content and a positive experience for viewers and advertisers. Here's a comprehensive overview of YouTube's monetization policies:

1. Eligibility Criteria: To be eligible for the YouTube Partner Program and monetization, your channel must meet the following criteria:

- Have at least 1,000 subscribers.
- Accumulate at least 4,000 watch hours in the last 12 months.
- Comply with all YouTube's policies and guidelines.

2. Content Guidelines: Your content must adhere to YouTube's Community Guidelines, which include rules about prohibited content, hate speech, harassment, violence, and more. Content that violates these guidelines may lead to demonetization or other penalties.

3. Advertiser-Friendly Content Guidelines: YouTube has advertiser-friendly content guidelines to ensure that ads appear on suitable and safe content. Avoid creating content that features sensitive topics, graphic violence, or controversial subjects that might hinder ad placements.

4. Copyright and Fair Use: Ensure that your content does not infringe on copyright laws. Using copyrighted material without permission may lead to demonetization or content removal.

5. Reused Content: YouTube's policies discourage the reuse of content that you don't own or have the rights to use. While using third-party content might not always lead to demonetization, original content creation is favored.

6. Metadata and Thumbnails: Use accurate metadata (titles, descriptions, and tags) that reflect your video's content. Misleading metadata, clickbait, and inappropriate thumbnails violate YouTube's policies and can impact monetization.

7. Engagement Manipulation: Do not engage in actions that manipulate views, likes, comments, or subscriptions, such as buying engagement or using deceptive tactics to artificially boost metrics.

8. User Safety and Misinformation: Create content that prioritizes user safety and avoids spreading misinformation. False information can lead to limited monetization or removal.

9. Children's Content: If your content is targeted at children, ensure compliance with the Children's Online Privacy Protection Act (COPPA) and related guidelines. Monetization may be affected in this category.

10. Review Process: Once you meet the eligibility criteria, YouTube reviews your channel's content for compliance with their policies. If your channel passes the review, you can start monetizing your videos.

11. Monetization Types: After being accepted into the YouTube Partner Program, you can earn through different revenue streams, including ad revenue, channel memberships, Super Chat, and Super Stickers.

12. Ongoing Compliance: Maintain adherence to YouTube's policies to retain monetization. Regularly review policy updates and make necessary adjustments to your content strategy.

Understanding and abiding by YouTube's monetization policies is crucial for maintaining a successful and sustainable channel. By creating high-quality, original content that respects the guidelines, you ensure a positive experience for both your viewers and advertisers, ultimately contributing to the growth of your channel's revenue.

Exploring Revenue Streams

Diversifying your revenue streams is essential for building a stable and sustainable income from your YouTube channel. Here are some revenue streams to explore beyond ad revenue:

1. Channel Memberships: Offer exclusive perks to subscribers who become channel members. These perks may include custom badges, emojis, members-only content, early access to videos, and special shoutouts during live streams.

2. Super Chat and Super Stickers: During live streams and Premieres, viewers can purchase Super Chats or Super Stickers to have their messages highlighted in the chat. Creators earn a portion of the revenue from these purchases.

3. Merchandise Shelf: Sell branded merchandise directly below your YouTube videos using the Merch Shelf feature. This includes items like clothing, accessories, and digital products that resonate with your audience.

4. Sponsored Content: Collaborate with brands and sponsors to create content that aligns with your niche. Sponsored videos can include product reviews, tutorials, or promotions. Be transparent with your audience about sponsored content.

5. Affiliate Marketing: Promote products or services in your video descriptions using affiliate links. When viewers make purchases through your links, you earn a commission.

6. Patreon or Membership Platforms: Set up a Patreon or similar membership platform to allow fans to support your channel with recurring monthly payments in exchange for exclusive content and perks.

7. Crowdfunding Campaigns: Use platforms like Kickstarter or Indiegogo to launch crowdfunding campaigns for specific projects or initiatives related to your channel.

8. Online Courses and Ebooks: Leverage your expertise by creating and selling online courses, ebooks, or digital resources that provide value to your audience.

9. Licensing Your Content: License your videos for use in other media, such as TV shows, commercials, or documentaries. This can generate additional income from your existing content.

10. Public Speaking and Workshops: If your channel establishes you as an expert in a specific field, consider offering public speaking engagements, workshops, or consulting services.

11. YouTube Premium Revenue: Earn a portion of the revenue generated from YouTube Premium subscribers who watch your content without ads. Your channel needs to be a part of the YouTube Partner Program to access this revenue stream.

12. Fan Funding Platforms: Platforms like Buy Me a Coffee allow fans to make one-time donations to support your work.

13. Live Events and Meetups: Host live events, workshops, or meetups for your audience. Ticket sales and merchandise from these events can contribute to your revenue.

14. Licensing Music: If you create music for your videos, you can license your tracks to other creators, filmmakers, or content producers.

By exploring these revenue streams, you can build a diversified income that reduces reliance on a single source. However, it's essential to ensure that each revenue stream aligns with your content and provides value to your audience. Balance the pursuit of revenue with maintaining the authenticity and quality of your content, as this is what keeps your audience engaged and invested in your channel.

Diversifying Income Through Merchandise and Sponsored Content

Two powerful ways to diversify your income on YouTube are through branded merchandise and sponsored content. These revenue streams allow you to monetize your creativity while providing value to your audience and partners. Here's how to effectively leverage merchandise and sponsored content:

Branded Merchandise:

1. **Design Relevant Merchandise:** Create merchandise that resonates with your audience and aligns with your content. This could include clothing, accessories, stickers, or even digital products like ebooks or presets.
2. **Quality and Design:** Ensure the quality of your merchandise matches your brand's image. Invest in well-designed and durable items that your audience would be proud to wear or use.
3. **Choose a Platform:** Use platforms like Teespring, Spreadshirt, or Printful to create and sell your merchandise. These platforms handle production, shipping, and customer service.

4. **Promote Creatively:** Promote your merchandise in your videos, on your channel page, and across social media. Create engaging content that showcases your merchandise in action.
5. **Limited Editions:** Consider offering limited-edition merchandise to create a sense of urgency and exclusivity among your audience.
6. **Engage with Feedback:** Listen to your audience's feedback on merchandise. Adapt and improve your designs based on their preferences.

Sponsored Content:

1. **Relevance and Alignment:** Partner with brands that align with your channel's niche and values. Choose products or services that genuinely benefit your audience.
2. **Transparency:** Clearly disclose when a video includes sponsored content. Maintain transparency to build trust with your audience.
3. **Authentic Integration:** Integrate sponsored products or services seamlessly into your content. Avoid creating overtly promotional videos that may turn off viewers.
4. **Provide Value:** Ensure that your sponsored content provides value to your audience. Offer insights, demonstrations, or reviews that help viewers make informed decisions.
5. **Negotiate Terms:** When negotiating with brands, consider factors like compensation, deliverables, exclusivity, and creative freedom.
6. **Long-Term Relationships:** Foster long-term relationships with brands that appreciate your content and consistently deliver value to your audience.
7. **Creative Freedom:** Maintain creative control over your videos. Work with brands that allow you to infuse your unique style into the content.
8. **Consistent Audience Experience:** Ensure that the tone and quality of your sponsored content match your regular content. Consistency is key to retaining your audience's trust.

Maintaining a Balance Between Monetization and Content Quality

1. **Value First:** Prioritize creating valuable content that resonates with your audience. Monetization should enhance, not compromise, the viewer experience.
2. **Content Authenticity:** Maintain your content's authenticity and originality, even when integrating revenue streams. Your audience values genuine engagement.
3. **Disclose Partnerships:** Clearly disclose any paid promotions or sponsorships in your videos to maintain transparency with your audience.

Adapting to Changes and Experimentation

1. **Stay Informed:** YouTube's monetization policies and algorithms may change over time. Stay informed about updates to ensure compliance and optimization.
2. **Experiment and Innovate:** Continuously experiment with different revenue streams and strategies. Adapt to your audience's preferences and changing trends.

Balancing Your Passion and Monetization Goals

Monetizing your channel offers exciting opportunities, but remember that the passion for your content remains at the core. Focus on creating content that resonates with your audience, and approach monetization as a means to sustain and enhance your creative journey. By diversifying your income streams and staying adaptable, you can create a stable foundation for the long-term success of your YouTube channel.

Chapter 13: Analyzing Performance and Growth

Analyzing your YouTube channel's performance is crucial for making informed decisions and driving growth. In this chapter, we'll explore how to effectively use YouTube Analytics to track progress, identify trends in viewer behavior, and adjust your content strategy based on valuable insights.

Using YouTube Analytics to Track Progress

1. **Access YouTube Analytics:** Go to your YouTube Studio dashboard and navigate to the Analytics section to access a wealth of data about your channel's performance.
2. **Overview Metrics:** Review key metrics such as views, watch time, subscribers, and engagement to understand your channel's overall performance.
3. **Audience Demographics:** Gain insights into your audience's age, gender, location, and interests. Use this information to tailor your content to your target audience.
4. **Traffic Sources:** Understand where your traffic is coming from – whether it's from YouTube search, suggested videos, external websites, or social media.

Identifying Trends and Patterns in Viewer Behavior

1. **Content Performance:** Analyze the performance of individual videos. Identify which videos have the highest views, watch time, and engagement.
2. **Viewership Patterns:** Determine when your audience is most active and adjust your content release schedule to maximize visibility.
3. **Audience Retention:** Examine audience retention data to identify the specific points in your videos where viewers tend to drop off. Use this insight to improve content flow.

4. **Top-performing Content:** Identify the types of content that consistently resonate with your audience. Replicate successful content formats while adding your unique touch.

Adjusting Your Strategy Based on Insights

1. **Content Evolution:** Use insights from Analytics to evolve your content strategy. Focus on creating content that aligns with audience preferences and watch patterns.
2. **Engagement Analysis:** Pay attention to which videos generate the most engagement, such as likes, comments, and shares. Aim to replicate this level of interaction.
3. **Keyword and Tag Optimization:** Use search term data to optimize your video titles, descriptions, and tags for better discoverability.
4. **Experimentation:** Based on insights, experiment with new content formats, styles, or themes while staying true to your channel's identity.
5. **Quality Improvement:** Continuously enhance video quality, production values, and storytelling techniques to keep viewers engaged.
6. **Collaborations and Trends:** Monitor trends in your niche and consider collaborating with other creators to tap into new audiences and fresh perspectives.
7. **Feedback Integration:** If viewers provide feedback in comments or surveys, use that information to fine-tune your content strategy.
8. **Long-term Planning:** Plan content and promotions based on anticipated trends, holidays, and special events.

Analyzing your channel's performance and making data-driven decisions is a fundamental aspect of YouTube success. By utilizing YouTube Analytics to its fullest, identifying trends in viewer behavior, and adjusting your strategy accordingly, you can create content that resonates with your audience, enhances engagement, and drives consistent growth over time.

Chapter 14: Overcoming Challenges and Staying Motivated

Navigating the challenges of maintaining a successful YouTube channel requires resilience and a strong sense of motivation. In this chapter, we'll explore strategies for overcoming challenges, managing burnout, and finding inspiration to ensure your continued growth and success.

Dealing with Algorithm Changes and Fluctuations

1. **Stay Informed:** Keep up-to-date with YouTube's algorithm changes through official announcements and industry updates.
2. **Diversify Content:** Create a variety of content to reduce the impact of algorithm shifts on your channel. Experiment with different formats and topics.
3. **Consistency Matters:** Consistent content creation and engagement help maintain a stable presence on viewers' feeds.
4. **Analyze Data:** Use YouTube Analytics to understand how algorithm changes affect your channel. Adjust your strategy accordingly.

Managing Burnout and Creative Blocks

1. **Set Realistic Goals:** Avoid overwhelming yourself with unrealistic expectations. Set achievable goals that align with your resources and schedule.
2. **Take Breaks:** Regularly schedule breaks to prevent burnout. Time away from content creation can lead to fresh perspectives and renewed creativity.
3. **Practice Self-Care:** Prioritize your physical and mental well-being. Engage in activities that rejuvenate you outside of YouTube.
4. **Seek Support:** Connect with fellow creators or a supportive community to share experiences and strategies for managing burnout.

Finding Inspiration to Keep Creating

1. **Explore Other Content:** Watch content from other creators, not only in your niche but also in unrelated areas, to spark new ideas.
2. **Read and Learn:** Read books, articles, and watch documentaries to expand your knowledge and gather inspiration from various sources.
3. **Stay Curious:** Embrace your curiosity and explore topics beyond your comfort zone. Unique insights can arise from unexpected places.
4. **Mind Mapping:** Use mind mapping techniques to visualize connections between ideas and generate new content concepts.
5. **Document Ideas:** Keep a digital or physical notebook to jot down ideas as they come. Review and expand upon these ideas when brainstorming.
6. **Engage with Your Audience:** Ask your audience for content suggestions or challenges they'd like to see you tackle.
7. **Creative Exercises:** Experiment with brainstorming exercises, such as word association or visual mood boards, to stimulate creativity.

Remember that challenges are a natural part of any creative journey. Staying motivated and overcoming obstacles requires a combination of adaptability, self-care, and a genuine passion for your content. By embracing change, managing burnout, and consistently seeking inspiration, you'll maintain a dynamic and engaging presence on YouTube while enjoying the creative process.

Chapter 15: Scaling Your YouTube Presence

As your YouTube channel gains traction, it's important to explore strategies for scaling your presence while maintaining quality and consistency. This chapter delves into methods for expanding your content offerings, outsourcing tasks, and creating a brand that extends beyond YouTube.

Expanding Your Content Offerings

Diversifying your content offerings can attract new audiences, keep your current viewers engaged, and position you as a versatile creator. Here's how to effectively expand your content on YouTube:

1. Experiment with Different Formats: Explore various content formats to keep your channel fresh and interesting. Some options to consider include:

- **Tutorials:** Share your expertise and teach your viewers new skills.
- **Vlogs:** Offer glimpses into your daily life or behind-the-scenes moments.
- **Q&A Sessions:** Engage with your audience by answering their questions.
- **Interviews:** Collaborate with experts, influencers, or other creators for insightful conversations.
- **Educational Series:** Create in-depth series that dive into specific topics.

2. Cover Related Topics: Expand into related niches or subtopics that align with your core content. For example, if your channel is about cooking, you could explore videos about kitchen equipment reviews, meal planning, or different cuisines.

3. Address Trends and Challenges: Stay relevant by incorporating trending topics, challenges, or viral content into your channel. This can attract new viewers who are interested in current discussions.

4. Geographic and Cultural Exploration: If feasible, explore content that focuses on different cultures, regions, or countries. This can expand your global audience and offer unique perspectives.

5. Collaborate with Others: Team up with other creators to collaborate on videos or series. This exposes your channel to their audience, helping you gain new subscribers.

6. Document Personal Growth: Share your journey and personal growth experiences. Whether it's fitness, self-improvement, or learning a new skill, your audience can learn alongside you.

7. User-Generated Content: Encourage your viewers to submit their content, stories, or experiences related to your niche. This fosters a sense of community and engagement.

8. Incorporate Entertainment: Integrate entertainment elements like challenges, skits, or parodies to diversify your content and provide a fresh perspective.

9. How-to Guides and Step-by-Step Tutorials: Guide your viewers through detailed processes, DIY projects, or creative endeavors relevant to your niche.

10. Educational Explainers: Create videos that explain complex concepts, industry trends, or current events in an accessible and informative manner.

11. Storytelling and Narratives: Share personal stories, anecdotes, or experiences that resonate with your audience and offer a deeper connection.

12. Product Reviews and Comparisons: Review products or services relevant to your niche and compare different options to help viewers make informed decisions.

13. Challenge Yourself: Set personal challenges or goals related to your niche and document your progress. This can inspire your viewers to take on similar challenges.

Remember that while diversifying your content can attract new audiences, maintaining a consistent brand identity is key. Ensure that the new content aligns with your channel's overall theme and resonates with your existing viewers. By expanding your content offerings thoughtfully, you can capture a wider audience while maintaining the authenticity that attracted your viewers in the first place.

Outsourcing Tasks as Your Channel Grows:

Outsourcing tasks can help you manage the increasing demands of your growing YouTube channel. Leveraging both agencies and tools can enhance your efficiency and overall content quality. Here's how to effectively delegate tasks with the help of agencies and tools:

1. Identify Tasks to Outsource: Determine which tasks are time-consuming or outside your expertise. Common tasks to outsource include video editing, thumbnail design, SEO optimization, social media management, and analytics tracking.

2. Consider Outsourcing Agencies: Agencies offer specialized services and a team of professionals. Consider these options for specific tasks:

- **Video Editing:** Partner with video editing agencies that specialize in creating engaging content.
- **Thumbnail Design:** Collaborate with graphic design agencies to create eye-catching thumbnails.

- **SEO and Analytics:** Work with agencies that provide SEO optimization and analytics insights.

3. Freelancers and Platforms: Websites like Upwork, Fiverr, and Freelancer allow you to hire individual freelancers for specific tasks.

4. Tools to Enhance Efficiency: Use tools and software to streamline processes and improve content quality:

- **Video Editing Tools:** Software like Adobe Premiere Pro, Final Cut Pro, or DaVinci Resolve for video editing.
- **Thumbnail Design Tools:** Canva or Adobe Spark for creating professional thumbnails.
- **Social Media Management Tools:** Buffer, Hootsuite, or Later for scheduling and managing social media posts.
- **SEO Tools:** SEMrush, Ahrefs, or TubeBuddy for optimizing video titles, descriptions, and tags.
- **Project Management Tools:** Asana, Trello, or Monday for tracking tasks and collaborating with freelancers.

5. Selecting Agencies and Freelancers: When choosing agencies or freelancers, consider their portfolio, expertise, rates, and reviews from previous clients. Ensure they align with your brand's values and goals.

6. Communicate Expectations Clearly: Provide detailed guidelines, deadlines, and examples when briefing agencies or freelancers. Clear communication is essential to achieving desired results.

7. Test and Review: Start with a smaller task to test the agency's or freelancer's capabilities. Review their work, provide feedback, and adjust the process as needed.

8. Maintain Consistency: Establish guidelines for brand consistency and style to ensure outsourced content aligns with your overall channel identity.

9. Budget Considerations: Balancing costs is important. Agencies may offer comprehensive services but at a higher cost, while freelancers or tools might be more budget-friendly.

10. Continuous Monitoring and Adjustments: Regularly assess the impact of outsourcing on your content quality, engagement, and overall growth. Adjust your approach based on the results.

By effectively leveraging outsourcing agencies and tools, you can maintain content quality, reduce your workload, and focus on tasks that contribute directly to your channel's success. Whether you choose specialized agencies or individual freelancers, the goal is to create a collaborative ecosystem that enhances your content and supports your channel's growth.

Creating a Brand Beyond YouTube

Expanding your brand beyond YouTube allows you to connect with your audience on various platforms and establish a more comprehensive online presence. Here's how to effectively extend your brand and create a broader impact:

1. Develop a Multi-Platform Strategy: Extend your presence to platforms like Instagram, Twitter, TikTok, and Facebook. Adapt your content to each platform while maintaining a consistent brand voice.

2. Build a Personal Website: Create a website that serves as a hub for your content, offers additional resources, and showcases your portfolio, achievements, and collaborations.

3. Utilize Social Media: Engage actively on social media platforms to connect with your audience, share updates, and foster community engagement.

4. Launch a Blog: Start a blog where you can delve deeper into topics related to your niche. Blogs offer in-depth insights and can attract a different audience.

5. Offer Online Courses or Ebooks: Leverage your expertise by creating and selling online courses, ebooks, or downloadable resources that provide additional value to your audience.

6. Host Workshops and Webinars: Organize virtual workshops, webinars, or live sessions to educate and interact with your audience in real-time.

7. Collaborate with Influencers: Collaborate with influencers or creators from different platforms to expand your reach and tap into new audiences.

8. Attend and Speak at Events: Participate in industry events, conferences, and workshops. Speaking engagements can position you as an authority in your niche.

9. Launch a Podcast: Create a podcast where you discuss relevant topics, interview experts, or share your insights in audio format.

10. Brand Partnerships: Collaborate with brands or companies for sponsored content, ambassadorships, or co-branded campaigns.

11. Offer Merchandise: Design and sell merchandise that reflects your brand's identity, giving your audience a tangible way to connect with your content.

12. Email Newsletter: Start an email newsletter to keep your audience updated with exclusive content, announcements, and insights.

13. Publishing: Consider writing a book, contributing articles to publications, or creating content for other platforms to expand your reach.

14. Charity Initiatives: Engage in charitable projects or causes that resonate with your brand values. This not only helps the community but also enhances your brand's reputation.

15. Consistency and Branding: Maintain a consistent brand voice, visual identity, and values across all platforms to create a cohesive and recognizable brand.

Scaling your YouTube presence requires careful planning and a strategic approach. As you expand your content offerings, engage professionals to assist with tasks, and create a brand presence beyond YouTube, remember to uphold the authenticity and quality that have contributed to your success. By staying true to your audience and continually innovating, you can effectively scale your presence while maintaining a strong connection with your viewers.

Chapter 16: Case Studies: Successful YouTubers' Journeys

In this chapter, we'll delve into inspiring case studies of well-known YouTubers who have achieved remarkable success. These stories showcase the diverse paths creators have taken to build thriving channels and offer valuable insights into their strategies, challenges, and achievements.

1. Case Study: PewDiePie (Felix Kjellberg):

- **Background:** PewDiePie is one of the most renowned YouTubers, known for his gaming content and comedic approach.
- **Journey:** Starting with gaming commentary videos, PewDiePie evolved his content to include humor, vlogs, and commentary on trending topics.
- **Key Takeaways:** Consistency, embracing trends, and connecting with his audience through authenticity have contributed to his massive following.

2. Case Study: Lilly Singh (Superwoman):

- **Background:** Lilly Singh is a comedian and motivational speaker who transitioned from creating humorous skits to inspiring content.
- **Journey:** Lilly's unique storytelling and relatable content resonated with audiences, helping her grow and even transition to late-night TV.
- **Key Takeaways:** Authenticity, relatability, and evolving content based on audience feedback led to her success.

3. Case Study: Mark Rober:

- **Background:** Mark Rober is an engineer who creates educational and entertaining science and engineering videos.
- **Journey:** His dedication to high-quality visuals, captivating experiments, and engaging explanations propelled his channel's popularity.

- **Key Takeaways:** Merging education with entertainment, focusing on unique content, and maintaining a genuine enthusiasm for the subject matter are crucial.

4. Case Study: Emma Chamberlain:

- **Background:** Emma Chamberlain is known for her relatable and comedic vlogs, often focusing on everyday life experiences.
- **Journey:** Emma's unfiltered and candid style resonated with Gen Z, catapulting her to popularity and influencing vlogging trends.
- **Key Takeaways:** Authenticity, catering to a specific audience demographic, and adapting content to current trends can lead to rapid growth.

5. Case Study: Linus Tech Tips (Linus Sebastian):

- **Background:** Linus Tech Tips is a channel focused on technology reviews, tutorials, and PC building.
- **Journey:** Linus started small, gradually building expertise and credibility in the tech community, resulting in a highly respected channel.
- **Key Takeaways:** Niche expertise, in-depth content, and building a loyal community can lead to sustainable growth.

These case studies exemplify the diverse strategies and approaches that successful YouTubers have taken to achieve recognition and build their channels. While each journey is unique, common themes include authenticity, consistency, adapting to audience preferences, and maintaining a strong connection with viewers. As you embark on your YouTube journey, studying these successful creators can provide valuable insights and inspiration to shape your own path to success.

Lessons Learned from Successful YouTubers' Experiences:

The journeys of successful YouTubers offer valuable insights that can guide aspiring creators towards their own paths of achievement. Here are lessons learned from the experiences of prominent YouTubers:

1. Authenticity Is Key:

Successful creators stay true to themselves and their unique style. Authenticity resonates with audiences and fosters genuine connections.

2. Consistency Yields Results:

Regularly uploading content builds anticipation and keeps your audience engaged. Consistency establishes trust and keeps viewers coming back for more.

3. Adapt to Changing Trends:

Staying up-to-date with current trends and adapting your content accordingly can attract new audiences and maintain relevance.

4. Engage with Your Audience:

Interaction with your audience, responding to comments, and incorporating their feedback help build a loyal community.

5. Quality Trumps Quantity:

High-quality content that provides value is more impactful than producing a large volume of videos. Invest time in research, scripting, and editing.

6. Embrace Your Niche:

Embrace your niche or passion and create content that genuinely interests you. Passion is contagious and captivates viewers.

7. Evolve and Experiment:

Successful creators are open to evolving their content based on audience feedback and experimenting with new formats and topics.

8. Embrace Failures and Learn:

Setbacks are part of the journey. Learning from failures and adapting helps you grow as a creator and refine your approach.

9. Find Your Unique Voice:

Discover your unique voice and style that sets you apart. Distinguishing yourself attracts a dedicated audience.

10. Be Resilient and Patient:

Building a successful channel takes time. Be prepared for challenges, stay resilient, and remain patient as your efforts bear fruit.

11. Collaborate and Network:

Collaborations with other creators can introduce your channel to new audiences and offer fresh perspectives.

12. Experiment with Different Content:

Don't be afraid to diversify your content and explore new formats. Variety keeps your channel engaging and dynamic.

13. Value Community Over Metrics:

Prioritize fostering a supportive community over chasing numbers. A strong community contributes to long-term success.

14. Strive for Continuous Improvement:

Always seek ways to improve your content, skills, and knowledge. Growth is a constant journey.

By studying the lessons learned from successful YouTubers, you can gain valuable insights that inform your content strategy, help you navigate challenges, and guide your path to becoming a recognized and impactful creator.

Applying Strategies from Successful YouTubers to Your Own Channel:

1. **Authenticity:** Stay true to your unique voice and personality, building a genuine bond with your viewers.
2. **Consistency:** Regularly create and upload content to establish a reliable presence and keep your audience engaged.
3. **Adaptation:** Embrace trends and evolving interests, tailoring your content to meet your audience's changing preferences.
4. **Engagement:** Interact with your audience through comments, live streams, and social media to foster a strong community.
5. **Quality:** Prioritize producing valuable, well-crafted content that resonates with your viewers, even if it means fewer uploads.
6. **Niche Passion:** Focus on creating content you're passionate about, carving your niche and attracting like-minded viewers.
7. **Evolution:** Be open to experimentation and improvement, learning from feedback and adjusting your content accordingly.
8. **Resilience:** Embrace challenges as learning opportunities, staying committed and patient as your channel grows.

9. **Uniqueness:** Develop a distinct style that reflects your personality and sets your content apart in a crowded platform.
10. **Collaboration:** Collaborate with other creators to broaden your reach and bring fresh perspectives to your content.

By implementing these strategies, you can build a strong and engaging YouTube channel that resonates with your audience and paves the way for your own success.

Chapter 17: Ethics, Copyright, and Community Guidelines

Maintaining ethical standards, respecting copyright, and adhering to YouTube's community guidelines are essential aspects of building a responsible and reputable presence on the platform. In this chapter, we'll explore the importance of ethical content creation practices, understanding copyright laws, and upholding community standards to create a positive and sustainable YouTube journey.

Respecting Copyright and Fair Use:

1. **Understand Copyright Basics:** Familiarize yourself with copyright laws to ensure you don't use copyrighted material without proper permission or attribution.
2. **Fair Use:** Learn about fair use guidelines, which allow limited use of copyrighted material for purposes such as commentary, criticism, news reporting, education, and research.
3. **Seek Permission:** Obtain permission from content creators if you plan to use their work in your videos, especially for commercial purposes.
4. **Give Proper Credit:** Always provide proper attribution to creators when using their content, whether it's images, music, or video clips.
5. **Create Original Content:** Focus on producing original content that showcases your creativity and avoids copyright infringement issues.

Maintaining Ethical Content Creation Practices:

1. **Be Truthful:** Ensure that the information you provide in your videos is accurate and fact-checked. Misleading viewers can damage your credibility.
2. **Respect Diversity:** Treat all individuals, communities, and cultures with respect and sensitivity. Avoid content that promotes discrimination, hate speech, or harm.

3. **Transparent Sponsorships:** Disclose any paid partnerships, sponsorships, or promotions in your videos according to legal and ethical guidelines.
4. **Avoid Clickbait:** Create titles, thumbnails, and descriptions that accurately represent the content of your video. Misleading clickbait can erode trust with your audience.
5. **Privacy and Consent:** Obtain proper consent from individuals before featuring them in your videos, especially if they're recognizable.

Upholding YouTube's Community Standards:

1. **Review Guidelines:** Familiarize yourself with YouTube's community guidelines and policies to ensure your content aligns with their standards.
2. **Respectful Comments:** Encourage respectful and constructive discussions in your comment sections. Monitor and moderate comments to prevent harmful interactions.
3. **Report Inappropriate Content:** If you come across inappropriate or violating content, report it to YouTube for review.
4. **Age-Restricted Content:** Use age-restriction when necessary to prevent minors from accessing content that may not be suitable for them.
5. **Demonetization and Strikes:** Understand YouTube's policies on content that could lead to demonetization or strikes on your channel. Avoid content that violates these policies.

By maintaining ethical content creation practices, respecting copyright, and adhering to YouTube's community guidelines, you create a safe, respectful, and responsible environment for both yourself and your audience. Upholding these principles not only fosters positive interactions but also protects your channel from potential legal and reputational risks.

Chapter 18: The Future of YouTube and Adaptation

In a dynamic digital landscape, embracing change and staying adaptable are crucial for sustained success on YouTube. This chapter explores strategies to navigate the ever-evolving trends, formats, and challenges that lie ahead, while emphasizing continuous learning and growth as a creator.

Embracing Evolving Trends and Formats:

1. **Stay Current:** Regularly monitor industry trends, platform updates, and emerging content formats to remain relevant.
2. **Experimentation:** Don't shy away from trying new video styles, formats, or platforms. Experimentation can lead to unexpected successes.
3. **Content Diversity:** Diversify your content offerings to cater to evolving audience preferences and reach a broader audience.
4. **Incorporate New Technologies:** Stay open to incorporating new technologies like virtual reality, augmented reality, or interactive elements into your content.
5. **User Engagement:** Engage with your audience to gauge their interests and feedback, helping you tailor content to their evolving expectations.

Staying Adaptable in a Rapidly Changing Landscape:

1. **Flexibility:** Be willing to pivot your content strategy as needed. Adapt to changes in algorithms, audience demographics, and platform policies.
2. **Feedback Loop:** Continuously gather feedback from your audience, analyze metrics, and adjust your approach accordingly.
3. **Resilience:** Embrace setbacks as opportunities to learn and grow. A resilient attitude enables you to overcome challenges.

4. **Industry Networking:** Connect with other creators, attend events, and engage in online communities to stay updated and share insights.

Continued Learning and Growth as a Creator:

1. **Skills Development:** Keep improving your skills in video editing, content creation, SEO, and audience engagement.
2. **Stay Curious:** Cultivate a hunger for learning. Research new topics, explore different niches, and expand your knowledge base.
3. **Adapt to Audience Feedback:** Listen to your audience's preferences, concerns, and suggestions. Adapting based on their input strengthens your connection.
4. **Explore Educational Resources:** Engage with online courses, webinars, and industry publications to stay informed about the latest trends.
5. **Personal Growth:** Invest time in personal development. Strengthen your public speaking, time management, and interpersonal skills.

As the future of YouTube unfolds, creators who embrace change, remain adaptable, and prioritize growth are positioned for success. By staying attuned to trends, experimenting with new formats, and committing to continuous learning, you'll not only thrive in the evolving landscape but also contribute to shaping the platform's future. Remember, YouTube rewards those who are proactive, adaptable, and committed to refining their craft.

Conclusion: Your Journey to YouTube Stardom

Congratulations on completing this comprehensive guide to starting and achieving success on YouTube! Your journey from an aspiring creator to a YouTube star is marked by dedication, learning, and consistent effort. As you reflect on the knowledge and insights you've gained, remember that your path to YouTube stardom is a continuous adventure.

Reflecting on Your Progress and Achievements:

Take a moment to appreciate how far you've come. Reflect on the skills you've developed, the challenges you've overcome, and the content you've created. Recognize your growth as a creator and the impact you've had on your audience.

Celebrating Milestones and Successes:

Celebrate each milestone you achieve along the way, whether it's reaching a certain subscriber count, receiving positive feedback, or hitting a view target. Recognize these accomplishments as stepping stones toward your larger goals.

Embracing the Ongoing Journey of YouTube Success:

Your journey as a YouTube creator is an ongoing process. Embrace the fact that success is not a destination but a continuous pursuit. Stay open to learning, adapting to changes, and refining your approach based on audience feedback and evolving trends.

As you move forward, remember that authenticity, quality, and genuine engagement with your audience are the cornerstones of a successful YouTube channel. Embrace the challenges, celebrate the victories, and enjoy the creative journey you've embarked upon.

Thank you for choosing this guide to accompany you on your path to YouTube stardom. Your dedication to your craft and your passion for creating content will undoubtedly lead you to great heights. Best of luck on your YouTube journey!

Appendix: Glossary of YouTube-Related Terms

1. Algorithm: The mathematical formula that determines which videos are recommended to users based on their viewing history, engagement, and preferences.

2. Analytics: Data and insights about your channel's performance, including views, watch time, audience demographics, and engagement metrics.

3. Audience Retention: The percentage of a video's length that viewers typically watch, reflecting how engaging your content is.

4. CTR (Click-Through Rate): The ratio of clicks to impressions for your video's thumbnail and title, indicating how well they entice viewers to click.

5. Demographics: Information about the age, gender, location, and interests of your viewers, helping you understand your audience better.

6. Monetization: The process of earning revenue from ads displayed on your videos, subscriptions, channel memberships, merchandise, and other income sources.

7. SEO (Search Engine Optimization): Techniques to improve your video's visibility in search results and recommendations, using keywords, titles, and descriptions.

8. Subscriber Count: The number of users who have chosen to receive updates when you upload new content.

9. Thumbnail: The image that represents your video and appears in search results and recommendations. A compelling thumbnail can increase clicks.

10. Tags: Keywords or phrases that describe your video's content, helping YouTube understand what your video is about and improving discoverability.

11. Watch Time: The total accumulated time viewers have spent watching your videos, a key factor in YouTube's algorithm.

12. Community Guidelines: YouTube's rules that creators must follow to ensure content is appropriate, respectful, and complies with legal and ethical standards.

13. Copyright: Legal protection for original creative works, preventing others from using your content without permission.

14. Fair Use: A legal doctrine that allows limited use of copyrighted material without permission for purposes such as commentary, criticism, news reporting, and education.

15. Content ID: YouTube's automated system to identify and manage copyrighted content in videos, allowing owners to block, monetize, or track their content.

16. Engagement: Actions viewers take on your videos, such as likes, comments, shares, and subscriptions.

17. End Screen: A customizable feature that appears in the last 5-20 seconds of a video, allowing you to promote other videos, playlists, or subscribe buttons.

18. Super Chat: A feature that allows viewers to pay to have their messages highlighted during live chat sessions, generating income for creators.

19. YouTube Partner Program (YPP): A program that enables creators to monetize their videos through ads, channel memberships, and merchandise.

20. YouTube Studio: The dashboard where creators manage and analyze their channel's performance, upload videos, and interact with the audience.

This glossary provides definitions for key YouTube-related terms to help you navigate the platform's terminology and concepts more effectively as you embark on your YouTube journey.

Recommended Resources and Tools for Creators

As you navigate your YouTube journey, these resources and tools can provide valuable insights, enhance your skills, and streamline your content creation process:

1. Online Courses and Learning Platforms:

- **YouTube Creator Academy:** Offers free courses on content creation, channel growth, and optimization directly from YouTube.
- **Udemy:** Features a range of courses on video editing, SEO, content strategy, and audience engagement.
- **Coursera:** Provides courses on storytelling, digital marketing, and social media strategies.

2. Books and Blogs:

- **"YouTube Secrets: The Ultimate Guide to Growing Your Following and Making Money as a Video Influencer" by Sean Cannell and Benji Travis:** A comprehensive guide to YouTube success.
- **TubeBuddy Blog:** Offers insights into YouTube best practices, algorithm updates, and audience engagement strategies.

3. Video Editing Software:

- **Adobe Premiere Pro:** A professional-grade video editing software with advanced features for creating polished content.
- **Final Cut Pro:** A popular choice among Apple users for high-quality video editing.

4. Thumbnail Design Tools:

- **Canva:** An intuitive platform for designing eye-catching thumbnails, banners, and social media graphics.
- **Adobe Spark:** Offers easy-to-use tools for creating graphics and videos, including YouTube thumbnails.

5. SEO and Analytics Tools:

- **TubeBuddy:** A browser extension that provides insights into keywords, tags, competitor analysis, and performance tracking.
- **VidIQ:** Offers SEO recommendations, keyword research, and data analysis for optimizing your videos.

6. Social Media Management:

- **Buffer:** Allows scheduling and managing social media posts across platforms to promote your content effectively.
- **Hootsuite:** Offers social media scheduling, monitoring, and analytics to maintain an active online presence.

7. Collaboration Platforms:

- **Zoom:** A video conferencing tool for remote collaborations, interviews, and live streams.
- **Google Workspace (formerly G Suite):** Provides tools like Google Docs, Sheets, and Drive for efficient collaboration and content planning.

8. Graphics and Animation Tools:

- **Adobe Photoshop/Illustrator:** Useful for designing channel banners, logos, and custom graphics.
- **Blender:** A free and open-source software for 3D modeling, animation, and visual effects.

9. Music and Sound Libraries:

- **Epidemic Sound:** Offers a vast library of royalty-free music and sound effects for enhancing your videos.
- **AudioJungle:** Provides a wide range of music tracks and audio assets for various video genres.

These resources and tools can help you refine your content creation skills, optimize your videos for discovery, and effectively engage with your audience. As you explore these options, tailor your choices to match your content's needs and your personal preferences.

Worksheets for Goal Setting, Content Planning, and More

These printable worksheets are designed to assist you in setting goals, planning your content, conducting research, and analyzing your progress on YouTube:

1. Goal Setting Worksheet:

- Clarify your short-term and long-term goals for your YouTube channel.
- Define specific, measurable, achievable, relevant, and time-bound (SMART) goals.
- Break down your goals into actionable steps and set target dates for each.

2. Content Planning Worksheet:

- Plan your video content for the upcoming weeks or months.
- Outline video ideas, titles, and brief descriptions.
- Allocate release dates and consider thematic groupings or series.

3. Keyword Research Worksheet:

- Research relevant keywords related to your niche or topic.

- Identify high-traffic keywords with search volume and low competition.
- Map keywords to specific videos in your content plan.

4. Video Optimization Checklist:

- Ensure each video is fully optimized for search and discoverability.
- Check off tasks such as optimizing titles, descriptions, tags, and closed captions.

5. Audience Engagement Tracker:

- Keep track of comments, likes, shares, and subscriber growth for each video.
- Analyze engagement patterns to understand what resonates with your audience.

6. YouTube Analytics Tracker:

- Record key metrics such as views, watch time, audience demographics, and top-performing videos.
- Compare data over time to identify trends and areas for improvement.

7. Collaboration Planning Worksheet:

- Plan and organize collaborations with other creators.
- Outline potential collaborators, content ideas, and contact information.

8. Social Media Promotion Plan:

- Map out your strategy for promoting videos on various social media platforms.
- Schedule posts, captions, and hashtags to maximize visibility.

9. Reflection and Improvement Worksheet:

- Reflect on the success of each video and your overall content strategy.
- Identify strengths, weaknesses, opportunities, and areas for improvement.

10. Video Monetization Tracker:

- Keep track of ad revenue, Super Chats, channel memberships, and other income sources.
- Monitor changes in revenue and analyze trends.

These worksheets provide a structured approach to setting goals, planning content, and monitoring your progress as a YouTube creator. Use them to stay organized, track your achievements, and refine your strategy over time.

1. **Email Marketing Subject Lines:**
   - Example: "Unlock 20% Off Your Next Purchase Today!"
   - Data: This subject line increased open rates by 30% and click-through rates by 15% compared to the average campaign.
2. **Social Media Captions for Engagement:**
   - Example: "Double-tap if you're excited for the weekend! □ #FriYay"
   - Data: This caption generated a 25% increase in likes and a 10% increase in comments compared to typical posts.
3. **Blog Post Headlines for Clicks:**
   - Example: "10 Must-Try Recipes for a Healthy Breakfast"
   - Data: This headline contributed to a 40% increase in click-through rates and a 20% increase in organic search traffic.
4. **Cold Outreach Email Templates:**
   - Example: "Hi [Name], I've Been Impressed by Your Work!"
   - Data: This personalized outreach template resulted in a 25% response rate from potential collaborators.
5. **Customer Testimonials for Trust-Building:**
   - Example: "Working with [Company Name] transformed our business. Sales increased by 50% in just three months!"

o Data: This testimonial contributed to a 15% increase in conversions on the company's website.

6. **Keyword Variations for SEO:**
   o Example: Targeting keywords like "best budget smartphones" and "affordable cell phones."
   o Data: These keyword variations led to a 20% increase in organic search traffic and higher rankings in search results.
7. **Call-to-Action Examples for Conversions:**
   o Example: "Claim Your Free eBook Now and Transform Your Finances!"
   o Data: This CTA generated a 35% conversion rate increase compared to previous CTAs.

1. **Design Inspiration for Creativity:**
   o Example: Using minimalist design principles for a website redesign.
   o Data: The updated design led to a 50% reduction in bounce rate and a 15% increase in time spent on the site.

1. **Content Idea Bank for Consistent Blogging:**
   o Example: A list of 50 blog post ideas, leading to consistent weekly content creation.
   o Data: This approach resulted in a 40% increase in blog traffic over a three-month period.
2. **Responses to Common Objections:**
   o Example: Providing well-crafted responses to common objections during sales calls.
   o Data: These responses contributed to a 25% increase in closing rates for new clients.

Remember that while these examples showcase successful outcomes, your results may vary based on your specific audience, industry, and approach. Adapt and customize these examples to suit your brand's voice and goals, and don't hesitate to experiment to find what works best for your unique situation.